D0905090

PF

DATE DUE

NOV 1 4 2007			
APR 2 9 2011			
			Printed in USA

HIGHSMITH #45230

The Library of the Nine Planets™

MERCURY

Carlo P. Croce

The Rosen Publishing Group, Inc., New York

Published in 2005 by The Rosen Publishing Group, Inc.
29 East 21st Street, New York, NY 10010

First Edition

Library of Congress Cataloging-in-Publication Data

Croce, Carlo P.
Mercury/by Carlo P. Croce.—1st ed.
   p. cm.—(The library of the nine planets)
Summary: Presents scientific discoveries about the atmosphere, size, surface, orbit, and rotation of the closest planet to the sun.
Includes bibliographical references and index.
ISBN 1-4042-0170-X (library binding)
Mercury (Planet)—Juvenile literature. [1. Mercury (Planet)]
I. Title. II. Series.
QB611.C69 2004
523.41—dc22

                                                        2003022402

Manufactured in the United States of America

On the cover: Image of Mercury taken by *Mariner 10.*

Contents

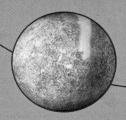

Mercury, one of the planets known to ancient man, still remains somewhat of a mystery. It was known of by the Sumerians, the ancient people who lived in Mesopotamia (modern-day Iraq) in the third millennium BC. The early Greeks and Romans also knew of Mercury as one of the five "wandering stars." Although Mercury's existence has been known *of* for thousands of years, little was known *about* the planet until recently. It wasn't until the mission of the spacecraft *Mariner 10* in 1974 that we got our first glimpse of the surface of this unusual planet.

Part of the reason we hadn't explored Mercury until recently is that its proximity to the Sun makes it hard to see from Earth. It only appears on the horizon just before dawn and just after dusk. This is a problem because looking at the planet on the horizon forces us to look at it on an angle through the atmosphere. The lower the planet appears in the sky, the more atmosphere we have to look through, which means more particles in the air get in the way and obstruct the light. This obstruction of light is what gives the sunrises and sunsets their beautiful colors. It's pretty, but it isn't practical when trying to study a planet.

Mercury's appearance both in the evening and morning led the ancient Greeks to believe it was actually two separate planets. As a result, they named the planet after their god Apollo when it appeared in the morning and after Hermes when it appeared in the evening sky.

Mercury, what we call the planet today, comes from the Roman name for the Greek god Hermes, the messenger of the gods. The planet's name possibly comes from the speed with which Mercury travels across the sky—Mercury moves faster than any other planet in the solar system.

Mercury is a fascinating planet. Although less than half of its surface was viewed by *Mariner 10*, most of what we know about this small, dark, elusive planet previously hidden in the glare of the Sun came from that very mission. Much more, however, remains to be uncovered. In 2004, the Mercury Surface, Space Environment, Geochemistry, and Ranging (*MESSENGER*) space probe will be launched to continue the exploration of this fascinating planet.

There is much to be discovered, not only on Mercury, but in the solar system as well. In March 2004, NASA announced the discovery of the "planetoid" Sedna, which orbits in the outer reaches of the solar system. Discoveries like these give us great hope that there is much more to be learned about the planets, our solar system, and the universe as a whole.

One

The History of Mercury

Ancient shepherds tending their flocks looked in amazement at the many celestial bodies in the night sky. Like a game of connect the dots, the ancients drew images by connecting the stars. The images were of warriors, gods, and animals. We call these images constellations.

Some of the "stars," however, appeared to wander from constellation to constellation. The word "planet" comes from the Greek word for "wanderer." One of these planets was called Stilbon by the Greeks and Gu-Ad by the Babylonians. We now call this planet Mercury.

An Interesting Past

Like many of the other planets, Mercury has been studied and written about since the beginning of recorded history. It stood as a figure in the mythologies of different civilizations and intrigued everyone who looked toward the heavens.

In Roman mythology, Mercury was the winged messenger of the gods, racing across the sky to deliver messages between the deities. No wonder the Romans named this planet Mercury.

Timocharis, a Greek philosopher thought to have been born in Alexandria, Egypt, around 300 BC, was the first person to record his observations of Mercury. Then, in 1639, the Italian

Mercury has been a prominent figure in the mythologies of many civilizations. In Roman mythology, Mercury was considered the winged messenger of the gods. It is believed that the planet Mercury was named after this god because of the speed at which it moves across the sky. Shown here is a painting of the figure Mercury from Roman mythology.

astronomer Giovanni Zupus (1590–1650) discovered that Mercury had phases, like our moon. This suggested that Mercury revolved around the Sun because the change in phases represents the movement of the planet.

In the late 1700s, Johann Hieronymus Schroeter (1745–1816), a German lawyer who later turned his attention to astronomy, was the first person to record details about Mercury's surface. In addition to preparing maps of Mercury's terrain, Schroeter said that

Mercury was a planet that might have an atmosphere. His findings, however, proved not to be accurate.

Italian astronomer Giovanni Schiaparelli (1835–1910) caused a great stir in astronomy by reporting markings on Mars and Mercury in 1877. He called these markings *canali*, or "canals." The concept of canals on Mars implied construction projects by intelligent beings beyond Earth and led to a search for life on other planets.

It was Schiaparelli's work that encouraged Percival Lowell (1855–1916), an American mathematician and astronomer, to build an observatory in 1894 to further investigate canals on Mars and Mercury. He built his observatory in Flagstaff, Arizona, and used his observations to prepare drawings of the surface markings of Mercury.

It was a mistake made by Giovanni Schiaparelli, shown here, that may have inspired our deeper understanding of Mercury. Thinking that *canali*, canals, were present on the planet drove Percival Lowell to build his famous observatory to map Mercury's surface, looking for intelligent life that could have built them. After further study, we now know the canals Schiaparelli thought he saw, in fact, do not exist.

In 1933, a French astronomer named Eugenios Antoniadi (1870–1944) charted the surface of Mercury in the most detail of the time. His maps were used by the scientific community for nearly fifty years. He used one of the strongest telescopes of his time and found that the canals on Mars and Mercury were not canals at all, but mistaken observations due to poor viewing conditions caused by Earth's atmosphere. For his contributions to the study of Mercury, a 280-mile-long (451 km long) ridge on the planet was named after him.

Science Imitating Religion

Before Johannes Kepler and the Polish astronomer Nicolaus Copernicus (1473–1543), people thought the Sun, stars, and planets revolved around Earth. This was consistent with the beliefs of the Catholic Church, which was very powerful at the time. The idea of Earth as the center of the universe with all bodies revolving around it was called the geocentric view of the universe (*geo* means "earth" and *centric* means "center").

When looking at the sky, however, astronomers noticed that the motion of the planets was strange. The planets moved across the sky, stopped, reversed direction, and then moved forward again. This was not consistent with the movement of celestial bodies that circled Earth. If they orbited Earth, these planets would move across the sky in one continuous path, like our moon.

So, in order to hold on to the church's beliefs, the concept of epicyclic motion was proposed. Basically, epicyclic motion stated that planets were revolving around imaginary points in space that were revolving around Earth.

Epicycles somewhat explained the motion of the planets, but not completely. To fully explain the strange phenomena and to keep the Catholic Church happy, epicycles within epicycles were proposed—anything to hold on to the notion of Earth as the center of the universe.

The theory of epicycles was eventually discarded once Kepler showed that Copernicus was right and the planets revolved around the Sun.

Johannes Kepler, shown here, was a major force behind the scientific revolution. During the revolution, new scientific discoveries were replacing religious explanations of how the universe worked. With Kepler's laws of planetary motion, the world finally had proof of the heliocentric model of the solar system, thereby disproving church doctrine.

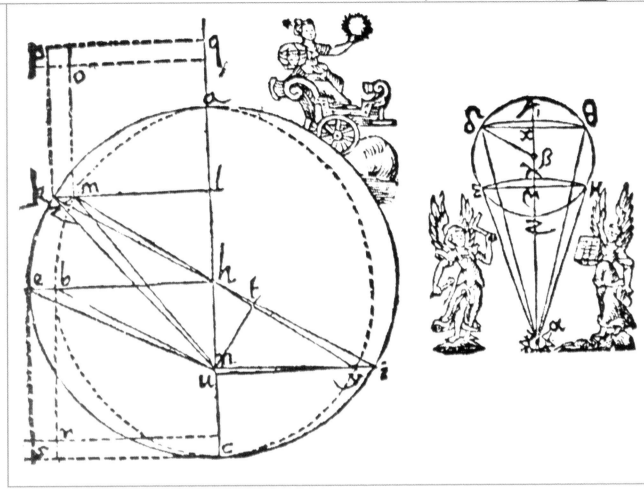

In addition to toppling the heliocentric model of the universe, Johannes Kepler also discovered laws of planetary motion that helped scientists calculate the position of Mercury at any given time. This helped later scientists study the planet and better understand its place in the solar system. Shown here is a page from Kepler's revolutionary book *Astronomia Nova* (New Astronomy), in which the laws were first uncovered. This particular diagram illustrates the elliptical orbit of Mars.

Between 1609 and 1618, the German astronomer Johannes Kepler (1571–1630) determined the orbital motion of the planets with his three laws of planetary motion, which calculated how the planets revolved around the Sun.

This discovery allowed Kepler to predict when and where Mercury would be in the sky, as well as when it would pass between Earth and the Sun. When the planet did pass between Earth and the

Sun, a phenomenon called transit, it could be seen as a small dot. Transit provided astronomers with a great opportunity to observe and learn about Mercury.

Finally, the German-born British astronomer Sir William Herschel (1738–1822), who discovered the planet Uranus in 1781, was the first to make serious telescopic observations of Mercury in the late eighteenth century.

Mercury has been an important figure in the histories of many civilizations and cultures. From its beginnings as the Greek wandering star, it has served as a central figure in Greek and Roman mythology. The discovery of Mercury's phases by Giovanni Zupus in 1639 suggested that the planets revolved around the Sun. Then Kepler's discoveries of planetary motion in the early 1600s supported this theory as well.

The theory that the planets revolved around the Sun was revolutionary because it was previously believed that Earth was the center of the universe. The discovery made people think that maybe they weren't the center of all things and that there was much more to learn about both Mercury and the universe.

Two

A Unique Planet

Mercury is the closest planet to the Sun. It is the tenth largest body in the solar system. Only Titan and Ganymede, the largest moons of Saturn and Jupiter, and the other eight planets except Pluto are larger than Mercury. Mercury's diameter is about 3,000 miles (4,880 km) or about the distance from New York to Los Angeles.

Mercury's dark, barren surface is covered with craters and looks like our moon. But unlike the Moon, Mercury is much denser, indicating that a large iron core sits beneath its thin rocky crust.

Mercury's gravity is 0.4 times that of Earth's, so a person weighing 150 pounds (68 kg) on Earth would only weigh about 60 pounds (27 kg) on Mercury.

The orbit of Mercury is the second most elliptical, or oval-shaped, orbit of the planets, second only to Pluto. This means that during Mercury's year, its distance from the Sun varies from 28 million miles (45 million km) at its closest point (called the perihelion) to 43 million miles (69 million km) at its farthest point (the aphelion). Depending on where Mercury is in its orbit, the Sun in Mercury's sky will appear two to three times bigger than it does in Earth's sky.

This isn't the only strange characteristic of the planet. Mercury's day is 58.6 Earth days long. Mercury's year is 88 Earth days long. This means that Mercury's day is approximately two-thirds the length of its year.

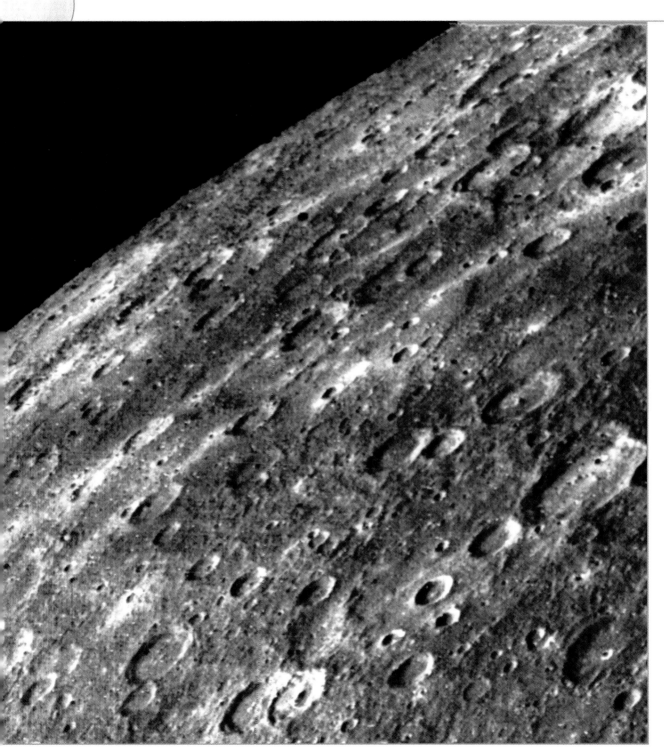

As a testament to just how far scientists have come since Schiaparelli and Lowell, this image, taken by *Mariner 10*, shows the surface of Mercury in fine detail. Due to its thin atmosphere that allows objects to reach the surface without burning up, Mercury is pockmarked with impact craters. Studied here is Wren Crater, visible at the lower center of the image. Running along the right side is Antoniadi Dorsum Ridge.

Another unique characteristic is that Mercury's axis has no tilt. This means that there are no seasons on Mercury, no time when the north or south poles are tilted toward the Sun, which is what causes the seasons on Earth. In 1991, radar observations showed that ice might exist deep in craters at the poles, which are shielded from the rays of the Sun because of this lack of tilt. The temperatures in the perpetual shadows can be as low as -180° Fahrenheit (-117° Celsius), which contrasts considerably with the sunlit surface, which can reach 950°F (510°C).

The Two-Year Day

Hundreds of years ago, humans measured time by the position of the Sun in the sky. The first simple clock was just a stick stuck in

Mercury Compared to Earth

	Mercury	Earth
Diameter	3,032 miles (4,880 km)	7,926 miles (12,756 km)
Rotation Period	1,407.6 hours	23.9 hours
Solar Day	4,222.6 hours	24 hours
Average Distance from Sun	36 million miles (58 million km)	93 million miles (150 million km)
Perihelion	28 million miles (45 million km)	91 million miles (147 million km)
Aphelion	43.4 million miles (69 million km)	94.5 million miles (152 million km)
Orbital Period	88 days	365.2 days
Orbital Velocity	29.7 miles/second (48 km/s)	18.5 miles/second (30 km/s)

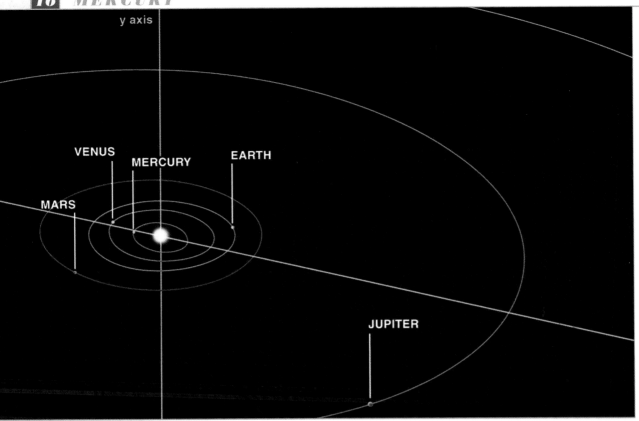

With accurate diagrams of the relative orbits of the planets, such as this, scientists are able to study the orbits in detail. Not only can scientists chart the planets' positions, but they can also calculate their orbital periods, velocities, and other characteristics involving their revolution around the Sun.

the ground. The shadow cast by the stick moved as the Sun moved. The moving shadow indicated the time of day. Twenty-four hours later, the stick's shadow was back in the same position.

This measurement of a day based on the position of the Sun in the sky is called a solar day—"solar" means "sun." A solar day here on Earth is twenty-four hours long. This means that it takes twenty-four hours for the Sun to arrive back in the exact same position in our sky.

But Earth does not take twenty-four hours to rotate on its axis. It takes only twenty-three hours and fifty-six minutes. The time it takes for a planet to rotate on its axis is called a sidereal day. The difference between a solar day and a sidereal day is due to a planet's motion in its orbit around the Sun. During the passage of one sidereal day, Earth moves 1/365th of the way in its orbit around the Sun. This movement of Earth causes the Sun's position in the sky to be shifted slightly from day to day. This means that it takes an extra four minutes for the Sun's position in the sky to catch up with where it had been the previous day. This is why there is a four-minute difference between Earth's solar day and sidereal day.

The difference between Earth's solar day and its sidereal day is very small and hard to notice. On Mercury, however, things are much different. Mercury rotates slowly on its axis. It takes 58.65 Earth days to complete its sidereal day. But the speed at which Mercury moves around the Sun is very fast. It takes only 88 Earth days for Mercury to orbit the Sun.

This means that during the time it takes Mercury to complete one sidereal day, the planet has traveled two-thirds of the way around the Sun. So, unlike Earth, which moves only a fraction of the way around the Sun during its sidereal day, Mercury has traveled nearly all the way around.

The Two-Sunset Day

As on Earth, the Sun on Mercury rises in the east. But instead of moving steadily across the sky to set in the west as it does on Earth, the Sun moves at varying speeds across the sky. It pauses, reverses direction, pauses again, and reverses direction again only to set in the west a year later. Then, after the Sun finally sets, it comes back again above the horizon and sets a second time!

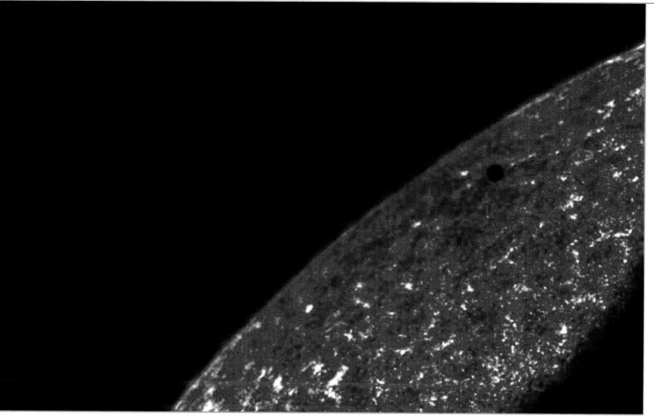

It is hard to imagine just how hot Mercury is unless you understand its position and size relative to the Sun. The fiery orb shown here is the Sun. The black dot at right center is Mercury. This image was taken on May 7, 2003, in a rare occurrence of "transit," or when a planet passes directly between Earth and the Sun.

Mercury's speed causes the Sun's position in its sky to change very rapidly. Because of the unusual movement of the Sun in Mercury's sky, it takes almost two years for the sun to wind up in the same position in the sky as it was the previous day. This means that Mercury's solar day is twice as long as its year.

Three

The Formation of Mercury

About 4.6 billion years ago, space dust and hydrogen gas began to come together. The dust and gas packed together, eventually forming the beginning of a star (protostar). As the protostar heated up and shrank from the gravity it exerted on itself, it began to rotate, similar to the way a spinning ice skater speeds up as he pulls his arms close to his body.

As the protostar rotated faster and faster, the surrounding gas and dust cloud flattened out into a disk. During this process, small particles throughout the disk collided and stuck to each other, forming larger particles. The more these particles collided, the larger the mass of particles became. Eventually, these particles grew into what are called protoplanets, bodies large enough to sweep up other smaller particles from the surrounding area. As these protoplanets became bigger, their gravity increased, allowing them to collect more and more smaller masses. One of these protoplanets was Mercury.

As the protostar increased in density, it continued to heat up. It finally reached a point where the heat and density were so great that it allowed atoms of hydrogen to combine. This process of atoms combining is called thermonuclear fusion, which releases immense amounts of energy. This thermonuclear fusion caused the protostar to ignite and become what we know of as the Sun. The heat from the new Sun vaporized the lighter particles in the inner solar system, and the solar wind

Shown here is a cutaway view of what scientists believe makes up Mercury's interior. The planet's large iron core is shown in yellow. Surrounding that is its thick mantle, in orange. To get a sense of the planet's size, the inset shows Mercury (the smaller planet) as it would appear placed next to Earth.

generated by the thermonuclear reaction within the new Sun blew away the remaining dust and gas. Only the heavier elements such as iron survived the Sun's heat. As a result, the planets that eventually formed closest to the Sun, such as Mercury, were made mostly of heavy metals such as iron and nickel.

During this time, the inner planets were so hot that they were in a molten state. In this state, the heavier elements such as iron and nickel settled to the center of the molten sphere. The lighter elements floated to the surface. This process of the lighter elements separating from the heavier ones is called differentiation.

As each planet cooled, the lighter materials on the surface hardened into a crust, surrounding the mantle of the planet. On Earth, the mantle floats on a molten iron core at the center of the planet. Sometimes the crust cracks, and the molten mantle seeps to the surface. This is what happens when a volcano erupts. Because Mercury is smaller than Earth, it cooled more quickly. Scientists think that Mercury's core is now solid.

Mercury's Magnetic Field

The diameter of Mercury's iron core is approximately 75 percent of the total diameter of the planet. This is the highest percentage of iron in the core of any of the planets. This makes Mercury the second densest planet in the solar system behind Earth. Mercury's mantle is only about 310 miles (500 km) thick.

Although astronomers feel that Mercury's interior is not hot enough now to keep its iron and nickel core melted, the planet does have a magnetic field, which is typically created by the movement of

An Interesting Forecast

Compared with the other planets, Mercury doesn't reflect that much of the Sun's light. There are some reflective surfaces, such as the light dust from more recent crater impacts, but Mercury's rocky surface generally absorbs most of the light. The absorbed sunlight becomes heat and adds to the extreme surface temperature of the planet.

On the dark side of Mercury, the temperature is about -281°F (-174°C). But because Mercury's day is so long, the temperature on the side exposed to the Sun can rise to 950°F (510°C). You could melt lead in the sunlight!

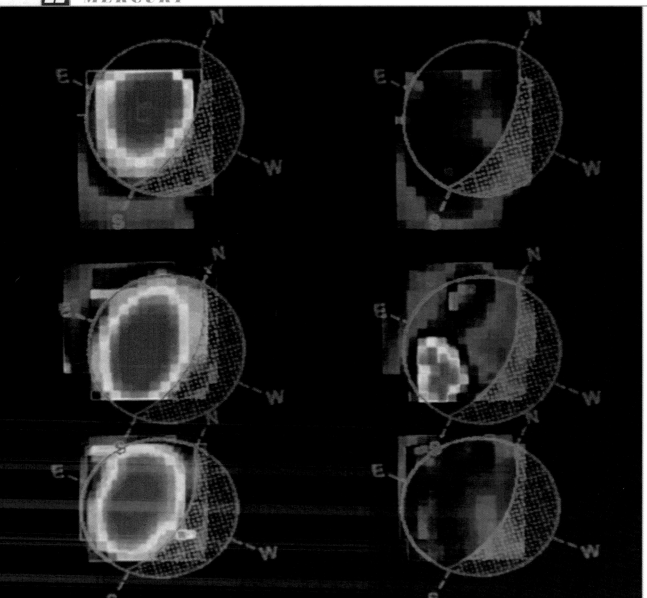

Scientists are very interested in Mercury's magnetic field. In this image, the three examples of Mercury at the left show its reflected sunlight. At the right, the examples show how sodium in the atmosphere is distributed around the planet over a three-day period. Sodium distribution is important because it tells scientists how Mercury's magnetic field influences its atmosphere.

a molten metal core. Some scientists feel that Mercury's magnetic field was created in the past when its core was molten, but as the planet cooled, the magnetic field was frozen into the solidified core, thus creating a permanent magnet.

Mercury's "Atmosphere"

Mercury has virtually no atmosphere. Because of the planet's small size, its gravitational force is only 0.4 times the strength of that on Earth. Because the gravitational force is so weak, there is not much gravity holding the atmosphere to the surface of the planet. So this weak gravitational force has allowed what little atmosphere Mercury had to escape the planet.

The vapors captured from the solar wind by Mercury's magnetic field, as well as the release of vapor from the planet's surface from meteorite impacts, have created a thin atmosphere. This thin atmosphere is continuously replenished by the release of vapor, but the vapor is almost immediately lost in space.

Mercury's Surface

Mercury's surface looks very much like that of Earth's moon. Large plains, pockmarked with impact craters, cover the planet. Some of these plains are relatively smooth, having been filled in by lava flow. The giant radio telescope in Arecibo, Puerto Rico, probing Mercury's previously unseen surface, shows a 53-mile-wide (85 km wide) crater and a lava flow extending some 560 miles (900 km) across.

Because of its small size, Mercury cooled faster than the other inner planets. This cooling shrank Mercury's diameter, causing cracks in its mantle. These cracks are called scarps. Some images of Mercury show impact craters cut by these scarps, indicating that some of these craters occurred before Mercury cooled and shrank.

One of the largest impact craters on Mercury is the Caloris Basin. (Any meteor crater larger than 125 miles [200 km] wide is typically called a basin.) The Caloris Basin measures 800 miles

The largest basin on Mercury, which is 800 miles (1,300 km) across, faces the Sun at its perihelion. Because of this, it was named Caloris, Latin for "hot." Shown here is the Caloris Basin taken by the *Mariner 10* spacecraft.

(1,300 km) across and was probably caused by an asteroid 60 miles (100 km) wide. The impact was so forceful that its shock waves tore up the terrain on the opposite side of the planet. The Caloris Basin filled with lava after impact.

The Presence of Water

Radar imaging of Mercury has shown that there may be water on the planet. The inside walls of deep craters at Mercury's north pole never see the light of the Sun, so the freezing temperatures there may allow ice to exist.

The strong reflections of radar waves from Mercury's north pole are similar in characteristic to ice reflections seen from Mars's icy polar caps. This water, if it does exist, could have come from past impacts with comets carrying ice from the outer limits of the solar system. More important, the presence of water offers the possibility that life as we know it may exist on Mercury, since water is necessary for the survival of living organisms.

Four

The Search for Planet Vulcan

Many of us enjoyed watching *Star Trek* on television and in the movies. The voyage of the spaceship *Enterprise* took us on a mission "to explore strange new worlds, to seek out new life and new civilizations, and to boldly go where no man has gone before." Spock, Captain Kirk's first officer, was from the mysterious planet Vulcan.

Of course *Star Trek*, Spock, and Vulcan were all fictional. But long before *Star Trek*, some astronomers were actually searching the inner realm of the solar system for a mysterious planet, which they called Vulcan. Why did they think such a planet existed? Well, it was because of Mercury's strange orbit.

Kepler and Planetary Motion

The shape of Mercury's orbit was first determined by Johannes Kepler when he observed the movement of the planets in the evening sky. Kepler revolutionized the study of the orbits of planets with his three laws of planetary motion, which he discovered from 1609 to 1618. These laws were revolutionary because they allowed future scientists to understand why certain planets like Mercury orbited the Sun as they did.

Kepler came up with these laws by studying the data on the position of Mars made by Kepler's mentor, the Danish astronomer Tycho Brahe. These laws became the foundation of

Leonard Nimoy, shown here, played Spock on the television show *Star Trek*. In the show, Spock was born in Shi'Kahr on the planet Vulcan. Vulcan was a mysterious planet in *Star Trek*. Many years before *Star Trek*, however, scientists used Vulcan as the name of the planet whose gravity they believed was affecting the orbit of Mercury.

modern astrophysics, which is the study of the physics of space. Simply stated, the laws are as follows:

- First Law: The planets orbit the Sun in elliptical orbits, or orbits shaped like ovals.

- Second Law: The speed of the planet changes as it orbits the Sun. The planet moves faster as it comes closer to the Sun and slower as it moves away from the Sun.

- Third Law: The time it takes for the planet to orbit the Sun is related to how far away it is from the Sun.

Isaac Newton

Sir Isaac Newton (1642–1727), using his newly invented mathematics called calculus, was able to predict the motion of the planets as they traveled around the Sun. Newton's calculations were very accurate except for one thing. Newton noticed that Mercury had an unusual and unpredictable orbit. Astronomers noticed that each time Mercury circled the Sun, its entire orbit would shift slightly.

Precession of the Perihelion

The perihelion in a planet's orbit is the point at which the planet is closest to the Sun. The gradual movement of the point with each successive orbit is called precession of the perihelion.

As Mercury orbits the Sun in its elongated elliptical orbit, the orbit itself slowly rotates. To better understand Mercury's precession of the perihelion, imagine that the Sun is the center of a clock. A line drawn from the Sun to Mercury at its closest point is the clock's minute hand. Each time Mercury orbits the Sun, this line connecting the Sun and Mercury at its closest point would be in a slightly different position, the way the minute hand of a clock moves slightly with each passing minute.

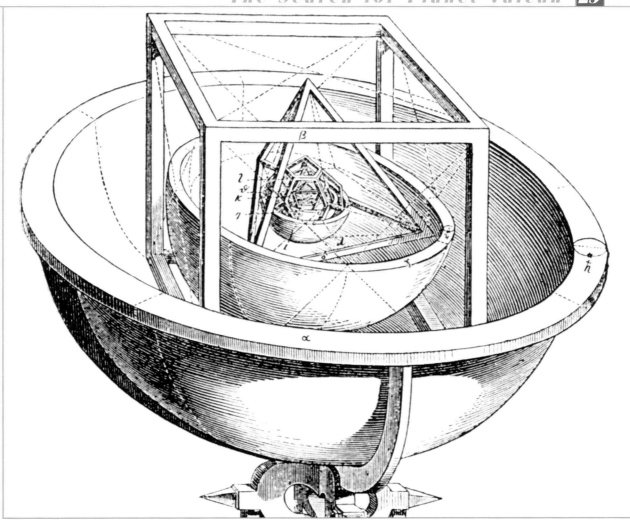

Explaining the orbits of the planets in Kepler's time was a difficult task. Scientists didn't have the instruments we have today to study the solar system. Shown here is one of Kepler's attempts to explain the solar system. This illustration of *Mysterium cosmographicum* (Cosmographic mysteries) shows Kepler's complex idea of the relationship between the orbits of the planets.

Imagine that Mercury is a race car and its orbit is the racetrack. The race car going around the track represents a planet traveling along its orbit. What Newton discovered was revolutionary. According to Newton, the path of Mercury around the Sun should be the same for each orbit. But it isn't. Mercury's orbit is slowly changing. It is as if the racetrack previously mentioned was turning each time the race car sped around it.

The career of one of the greatest scientists of the twentieth century was possibly established because of studies he conducted in researching Mercury. After studying the planet's precession of the perihelion, Albert Einstein, shown here, developed his concept of relativity. Einstein's theory of relativity is one of the most important scientific breakthroughs ever.

The technical name for this moving orbit is called precession of the perihelion. Scientists thought Mercury's precession of the perihelion was possibly caused by the gravity of some unseen planet, which they called Vulcan, pulling on Mercury.

Attempts were made to find Vulcan, and some astronomers mistakenly reported seeing the planet, but no such planet was ever found to exist. Without Vulcan, there was no explanation for the strange behavior of Mercury.

But then, in 1917, the German-born physicist Albert Einstein (1879–1955) published his paper called "Cosmological Considerations on the General Theory of Relativity." This paper outlined the new concept of relativity and changed the way scientists look at space. Part of Einstein's theory said that the gravity of celestial bodies actually warps or curves space and that the planets follow these curves when they move. This is similar to the way a bar of soap follows the current of the water near an open drain in the bathtub. Einstein went on to apply this principle to Mercury's mysterious orbit. Mercury, in this case, was the soap, the Sun was the drain, and the current of water was the curvature of space.

When Einstein's calculations for the curvature of space were factored into Newton's equations for Mercury's orbit, Mercury's precession of the perihelion was explained. So Mercury helped Einstein become one of the most famous scientists in history.

Five

Sailing into the Future

Between 1962 and 1973, the National Aeronautics and Space Administration (NASA) designed and built ten space probes to explore the inner solar system. These were named *Mariner*. They were small robotic explorers weighing around 1,000 pounds (453 kg) each.

Launched in November 1973, *Mariner 10* embarked on a two-year journey to Venus and Mercury. During this voyage, almost 12,000 images were taken of these planets. In 1974 and 1975, during three flybys of Mercury, *Mariner 10* was able to photograph almost half of the planet's surface. The spectacular images were the first to show terrain remarkably similar to our own moon.

One of the technical obstacles in the design of the *Mariner 10* mission was in dealing with Earth's speed in orbit. Since Earth travels at 66,000 miles per hour (106,000 km/h) as it moves around the Sun, everything on Earth is traveling at that speed. So a spacecraft traveling, let's say, 500 miles per hour (805 km/h) when launched from Earth is moving at that speed compared with Earth. But compared with the Sun, that spacecraft is going 500 miles per hour plus 66,000 miles per hour. So, in effect, the spacecraft is traveling at 66,500 miles per hour (106,999 km/h). That's pretty fast.

This immense speed causes a major problem in sending a spacecraft to Mercury. Since Mercury is closer to the Sun than

Mariner 8 was one of the ten space probes NASA built to study the inner solar system. Shown here before launch, *Mariner 8* is being fitted with solar panels. *Mariner 8* ultimately did not explore Mercury. It was scheduled to study Mars, but it did not even do that due to its launch failure on May 8, 1971. Its sister spacecraft *Mariner 10*, however, did reach Mercury, taking thousands of photos and mapping almost half of the planet's surface.

Earth, it needs to slow down to less than Earth's speed in order to fall into an orbit closer to the Sun than Earth. If the spacecraft traveled faster than Earth, it would move away from the Sun into an orbit outside that of Earth's. So the only way for the spacecraft to move closer to the Sun was to slow down to less than Earth's speed.

But how can you slow down a spacecraft? Even though *Mariner 10* was pretty light, the immense power needed to slow it down enough to drop into Mercury's orbit was beyond the capability of the rocket engines available at that time. So scientists devised a new plan called the planetary gravity assist.

The Gravity Assist

In the case of *Mariner 10*, the spacecraft could be slowed down only enough to get it to fly by Venus, which is closer to Earth and doesn't require as much power to reach. Scientists then used Venus's gravity to slingshot *Mariner 10* toward Mercury.

The concept is sometimes likened to playing billiards in space. *Mariner 10* was effectively bounced off Venus and into Mercury. Although the concept of gravity assist had been around for many years, the launch of *Mariner 10*, the last of the Mariner voyages, was the first time it was used.

Solar Wind

Solar wind is a stream of particles erupting from the Sun at speeds of up to 1,000,000 miles per hour (1,600,000 km/h). If you've ever seen a picture of a comet's tail, then you've seen the effect of solar wind. The tail of a comet only develops as the comet approaches the Sun, and it always faces away from the Sun. That is because the tail of the comet is the result of dust and ice particles being blown off of it by solar wind.

Mariner's Fuel

Mariner 10 used 64 pounds (29 kg) of liquid fuel on its trip to Mercury. It also relied on solar energy for power. The solar energy was made possible by two solar panels. These panels generated electricity from the sunlight that struck them. But these panels were also used as sails, capturing solar wind and guiding *Mariner 10* toward Mercury. When the probe's fuel ran low, the solar panels were positioned to act as sails to make course corrections.

The Discoveries of *Mariner 10*

Most of the information we know about Mercury today came from the *Mariner 10* mission. The space probe had three separate encounters with Mercury. The first occurred on March 29, 1974, when *Mariner 10* first fell within orbit of Mercury. It came within 500 miles (805 km) of the planet.

During this encounter, scientists got their first close-up view of an intensely cratered planet that resembles the Moon. After its first encounter with Mercury, *Mariner 10* entered an orbit around the Sun. This permitted *Mariner 10* to come back again and view Mercury two additional times.

The second Mercury encounter provided another opportunity to photograph the sunlit side of the planet and the south polar region from an altitude of about 30,000 miles (48,000 km).

On its third encounter on March 16, 1975, *Mariner 10* came within 200 miles (322 km) of the planet and took an additional 300 photographs. Magnetic field measurements were also taken.

On March 24, 1975, when gas that controlled its altitude depleted, *Mariner 10* was turned off. It was put into orbit around

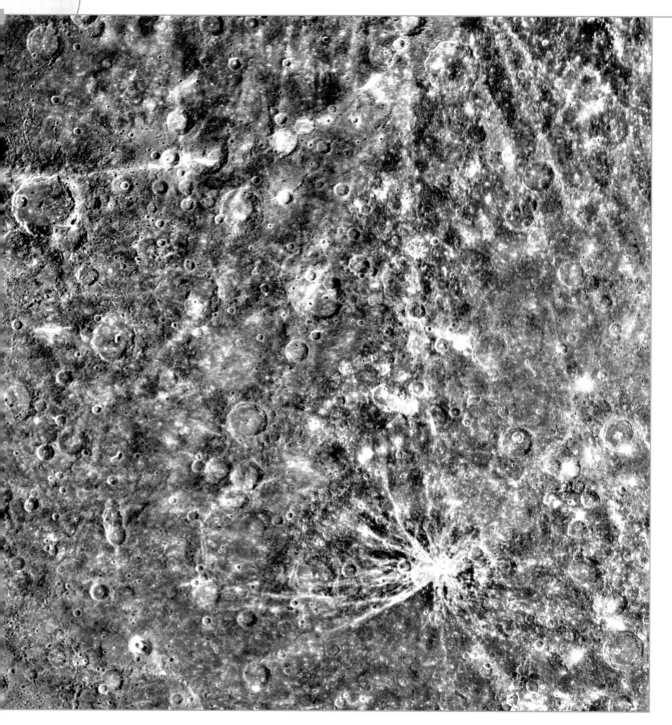

When *Mariner 10* flew by Mercury in 1974, it took thousands of photos of the planet's surface. This photo is of the Beethoven Quadrangle, named after the nineteenth-century German classical composer Ludwig van Beethoven. Scientists were surprised to learn that Mercury's surface, which is pockmarked with impact craters, resembles that of Earth's moon.

the Sun, where it has been circling ever since. The total cost of the mission was $100 million.

Mariner 10 provided a wealth of information about Mercury. The mission taught scientists that Mercury possessed a magnetic field and a relatively large iron-rich core. Scientists also learned that Mercury has a thin atmosphere composed mostly of sodium and potassium. Thousands of photos taken by *Mariner 10* allowed scientists to map almost 45 percent of the surface of Mercury.

Shown here in this artist's illustration, *MESSENGER* is a craft scheduled to study Mercury. *MESSENGER* will continue where *Mariner 10* left off, studying the planet's unique geologic characteristics. The *MESSENGER* mission will also allow scientists to prepare for the next mission, *BepiColombo*, which is scheduled to launch in 2011.

The *MESSENGER* Mission

In the summer of 2004, the spacecraft *MESSENGER* will be launched from Cape Canaveral, Florida. It will travel nearly 4 billion miles (6.4 billion km) before encountering and orbiting Mercury in 2011. Like *Mariner 10*, *MESSENGER* will use the gravity assist provided by Venus to help it get to Mercury.

This mission will add to the information obtained by *Mariner 10*. *MESSENGER* will gather extensive data on Mercury's geology, density, core composition, magnetic field, and atmosphere. To accomplish this task, *MESSENGER* will carry a wealth of scientific instruments along with backup systems to take over in the event of any system failures. Solar panels will generate electrical power from the Sun. This electricity will be stored in rechargeable batteries.

MESSENGER will continue to orbit and study the planet. *MESSENGER*'s orbit will allow it to circle the planet twice every twenty-four hours, and it will take it as close as 125 miles (201 km) above the surface of the planet. After the mission is complete, *MESSENGER*'s communications will cease, but the probe will continue to orbit Mercury for several years until it finally spirals down and crashes into the planet.

BepiColombo

BepiColombo is a Mercury space probe scheduled to be launched from the European Space Operations Center in Darmstadt, Germany, in 2011. It will embark on a three-and-a-half-year voyage of exploration of Mercury. The spacecraft was named after the Italian mathematician and engineer, Giuseppe "Bepi" Colombo, who, among other things, proposed using Venus's gravity to assist *Mariner 10* to Mercury.

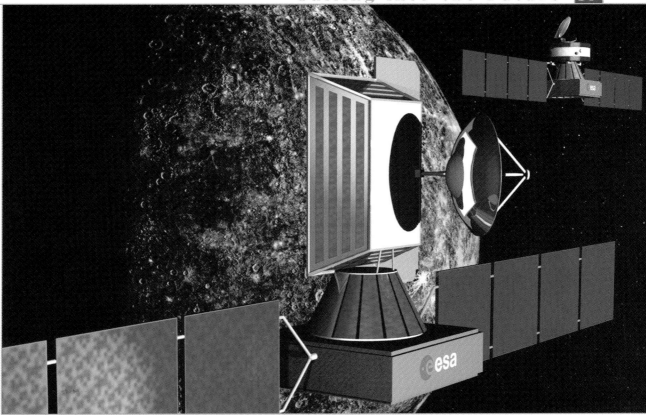

BepiColombo, which is scheduled to launch in 2011, will add to the discoveries made about Mercury by *Mariner 10* and *MESSENGER*. Circling Mercury for one year, *BepiColombo* will gather data and conduct experiments that will further scientists' understanding of the planet.

BepiColombo will circle Mercury for one year, gathering data and conducting experiments, including developing ways to detect asteroids that could strike Earth. After a year in orbit, the space probe will land on the planet's surface, where it will do soil analysis and measure any seismic activity.

Telescopic Images

One of the greatest technological developments in space exploration has been the Hubble Space Telescope, the first telescope in space. The telescope was named after the American astronomer Edwin Hubble, whose observations led to the theory that the universe is expanding.

The concept of a telescope in space was first proposed in 1946 as a way of overcoming the difficulties that Earth's atmosphere created in viewing distant stars. Finally built and launched in 1990, the Hubble Space Telescope was a catastrophic failure at first because of mistakes made when manufacturing its lenses. Scientists were not able to focus the telescope. Then, in 1993, astronauts fitted the Hubble with lenses that corrected the problem. The results were spectacular.

The Hubble Space Telescope has shown us amazing, never-before-seen views of the universe, which have been impossible to see with any telescope beneath the surface of Earth's atmosphere. Yet because of its powerful magnification, the Hubble is extremely sensitive to light. This sensitivity means that it cannot be pointed in the direction of the Sun. Because the direction of Mercury from Earth is toward the Sun, Mercury has never been seen through the Hubble.

Earth-based telescopes cannot see any detail on Mercury due to its proximity to the Sun. Both the Sun's glare and the atmosphere interfere with the viewing of the planet. However, researchers at Boston University have reported that advances in computer image enhancement of telescopic images of Mercury are allowing scientists to finally see the details of Mercury's surface. Who knows what mysteries of Mercury remain to be uncovered.

Circa 3000 BC: Mercury is observed by the ancient Sumerians.

1609–1618: German astronomer Johannes Kepler determines the orbital motion of the planets with his three laws of planetary motion, which allow him to calculate the dates that Mercury moves between Earth and the Sun.

1877: Italian astronomer Giovanni Schiaparelli first reports seeing canals on Mercury's surface. This leads to the belief that there is life on the planet.

1933: French astronomer Eugenios Antoniadi creates the most detailed map to date of Mercury's surface.

1974: *Mariner 10* falls within orbit of Mercury on March 29, getting the first close-up view of Mercury's craters.

2004: The spacecraft *MESSENGER* is scheduled to be launched. It travels nearly 4 billion miles (6.4 billion km) to Mercury.

2011: *BepiColombo*, a Mercury space probe, is scheduled to be launched from the European Space Operations Center in Darmstadt, Germany. It embarks on a three-and-a-half-year exploration of Mercury. *MESSENGER* reaches Mercury.

Circa 300 BC: Timocharis becomes the first person to record his observations of Mercury.

1639: The Italian astronomer Giovanni Zupus discovers that Mercury has phases, suggesting that the planet circles the Sun.

1894: American mathematician and astronomer Percival Lowell builds his observatory in Flagstaff, Arizona, from which he sketches the surface markings of Mercury.

1973: *Mariner 10* is launched in November and embarks on a two-year journey to Venus and Mercury.

1975: *Mariner 10* takes the first measurements of Mercury's magnetic field on March 16. It is turned off on March 24 and put into orbit around the Sun, where it has been ever since.

Glossary

aphelion A planet's farthest point from the Sun.

axis An imaginary line running through the poles of a planet around which the planet rotates.

basin A crater larger than 125 miles (200 km) wide.

density The amount of mass within a certain amount of space.

diameter The length of a straight line through the center of an object.

differentiation The process that separates lighter elements from the heavier ones in the molten core of a planet.

epicycle The process by which one planet orbits a second, while that second planet is orbiting a third.

gravity An attracting force between massive objects.

gravity assist The use of a planet's gravity to propel a spacecraft.

mass A measurement that consists of the amount of matter an object has.

orbital period The time it takes for a planet to revolve around the Sun once.

orbital velocity The speed at which a planet moves in orbit around the Sun.

perihelion A planet's closest point to the Sun.

protoplanet An accumulation of mass that forms the beginning of a planet.

protostar An accumulation of particles that will eventually become a star during the formation of a solar system.

scarp Cracks in the crust or mantle of a planet.

sidereal day The actual length of time for a planet to complete one full day while in orbit around the Sun.

solar day The length of a day determined by the position of the Sun in the sky.

thermonuclear fusion The coming together of atoms to form energy.

vaporize To become a gas.

For More Information

Lowell Observatory
1400 West Mars Hill Road
Flagstaff, AZ 86001
(928) 774-3358
Web site: http://www.lowell.edu

National Aeronautics and Space Administration (NASA)
NASA Headquarters, Information Center
Washington, DC 20546-0001
(202) 358-0000
Web site: http://www.nasa.gov

Smithsonian National Air and Space Museum
Seventh Street and Independence Avenue SW
Washington, DC 20560
(202) 357-2700
Web site: http://www.nasm.si.edu

Web Sites

Due to the changing nature of Internet links, the Rosen Publishing Group, Inc., has developed an online list of Web sites related to the subject of this book. This site is updated regularly. Please use this link to access the list:

http://www.rosenlinks.com/lnp/merc

For Further Reading

Asimov, Isaac. *Mercury* (Isaac Asimov's 21st Century Library of the Universe). Milwaukee, WI: Gareth Stevens Publishing, Inc., 2002.

Goss, Tim, *Uranus, Neptune, and Pluto* (The Universe). Portsmouth, NH: Heinemann Library, 2003.

Kerrod, Robin. *Mercury and Venus.* Minneapolis, MN: Lerner Publications Company, 2003.

McNab, David, and James Younger. *The Planets.* New Haven, CT: Yale University Press, 1999.

Strom, Robert G. *Mercury: The Elusive Planet.* Washington, DC: Smithsonian Institution Press, 1987.

Bibliography

Fradin, Dennis B. *The Planet Hunters: The Search for Other Worlds.* New York: Margaret K. McElderry Books, 1997.

Gallant, Roy A. *National Geographic Picture Atlas of Our Universe.* Washington, DC: National Geographic Society, 1986.

Hartmann, William K., and Chris Impey. *Astronomy, The Cosmic Journey.* Florence, KY: Wadsworth, 1997.

Mayall, R. Newton. *The Sky Observers Guide: A Handbook for Amateur Astronomers* (Golden Guide). New York: Golden Press, 1985.

McNab, David, and James Younger. *The Planets.* New Haven, CT: Yale University Press, 1999.

Index

A

Antoniadi, Eugenios, 9

B

Babylonians, 7
BepiColombo, 38–39
Brahe, Tycho, 26

C

Caloris Basin, 23–25
Copernicus, Nicolaus, 10
craters, impact, 23–25

E

Earth, 5, 9, 10, 11, 12, 13, 21, 23, 32, 33, 34, 39
  atmosphere of, 5, 9, 40
  orbit of, 16, 17
  seasons on, 15
Einstein, Albert, 31
epicyclic motion, 10

G

gravity assist, explanation of, 34
Greeks, 5, 6, 7, 12

H

Herschel, William, 12
Hubble Space Telescope, 39–40

J

Jupiter, 13

K

Kepler, Johannes, 10, 11, 12, 26

L

Lowell, Percival, 9

M

Mariner 10, 5, 6, 32, 34, 35, 38
  discoveries of, 35–37
Mars, 9, 25
Mercury
  atmosphere of, 9, 23, 37, 38
  axis of, 15
  core of, 21, 22, 37, 38
  early observations of, 5, 6, 7–8
  formation of, 19–21
  magnetic field of, 21–22, 35, 37, 38
  orbit of, 11–12, 13, 17, 26, 28–31, 34
  phases of, 8, 12
  size of, 13
  surface of, 8, 9, 13, 23, 32, 37, 40
  water on, 25
MESSENGER, 6, 38
Moon, the, 10, 13, 23, 32, 35

N

NASA, 6, 32
Newton, Sir Isaac, 28, 29, 31

P

perihelion, precession of the, 28, 30, 31
planetary motion, 10, 11, 12, 17, 28
  laws of, 26–28
Pluto, 13
protoplanets, explanation of, 19

About the Author

Carlo P. Croce is a retired package designer living in New Jersey.

Credits

Cover © U.S. Geological Survey/Science Photo Library/Photo Researchers, Inc.; pp. 4–5 NASA/JPL; p. 8 © The Bridgeman Art Gallery/Getty Images, Inc.; pp. 9, 10, 11, 30 © Science Photo Library/Photo Researchers, Inc.; p. 14 NASA/NSSDC; p. 16 NASA/Lunar and Planetary Institute; p. 18 NASA; p. 20 © Mark Garlick/Science Photo Library/Photo Researchers, Inc.; p. 22 © A. E. Potter/NASA/Science Photo Library/Photo Researchers, Inc.; pp. 24, 36 NASA/JPL/CalTech; p. 27 © Bettmann/Corbis; p. 33 NASA/Kennedy Space Center; p. 37 © NASA/Johns Hopkins University Applied Physics Laboratory/Carnegie Institution of Washington; p. 39 ESA.

Designer: Thomas Forget; Editor: Nicholas Croce